Vincent van Gogh

Quotes... Vol.28

by The Secret Libraries

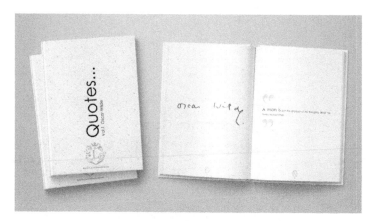

Kindle EDITION
Find us on:

The Secret Libraries

Published by The Secret Libraries for 2017
www.theSECRETlibraries.com

Quotes...

This book provides a selected collection of 155 quotes from the works of Vincent van Gogh.

Vincent van Gogh

1853-1890

I feel that there is nothing more truly artistic than to love people.

If you hear a voice within you say 'you cannot paint,' then by all means paint, and that voice will be silenced.

Love many things, for therein lies the true strength, and whosoever loves much performs much, and can accomplish much, and what is done in love is done well.

Great things are done by a series of small things brought together.

What would life be if we had no courage to attempt anything?

For my part I know nothing with any certainty, but the sight of the stars makes me dream.

I often think that the night is more alive and more richly colored than the day.

"

I put my heart and my soul into my work, and have lost my mind in the process.

"

I dream my painting and I paint my dream.

Be clearly aware of the stars and infinity on high. Then life seems almost enchanted after all.

...and then, I have nature and art and poetry, and if that is not enough, what is enough?

I put my heart and soul into my work, and I have lost my mind in the process.

Normality is a paved road: It's comfortable to walk, but no flowers grow on it.

Close friends are truly life's treasures. Sometimes they know us better than we know ourselves. With gentle honesty, they are there to guide and support us, to share our laughter and our tears. Their presence reminds us that we are never really alone.

The sadness will last forever.

What would life be if we had no courage to attempt anything?

"

The fishermen know that the sea is dangerous and the storm terrible, but they have never found these dangers sufficient reason for remaining ashore.

"

"

I am seeking, I am striving, I am in it with all my heart.

"

I try more and more to be myself, caring relatively little whether people approve or disapprove.

" If you truly love nature, you will find beauty everywhere. **"**

Great things are not done by impulse, but by a series of small things brought together.

It is with the reading of books the same as with looking at pictures; one must, without doubt, without hesitations, with assurance, admire what is beautiful.

The best way to know God is to love many things.

I am always doing what I cannot do yet, in order to learn how to do it.

Art is to console those who are broken by life.

If I am worth anything later, I am worth something now. For wheat is wheat, even if people think it is a grass in the beginning.

I want to touch people with my art. I want them to say 'he feels deeply, he feels tenderly'.

It is looking at things for a long time that ripens you and gives you a deeper meaning.

The beginning is perhaps more difficult than anything else, but keep heart, it will turn out all right.

Exaggerate the essential, leave the obvious vague.

There is the same difference in a person before and after he is in love as there is in an unlighted lamp and one that is burning. The lamp was there and was a good lamp, but now it is shedding light too, and that is its real function. And love makes one calmer about many things, and that way, one is more fit for one's work.

"

There is peace even in the storm.

"

I wish they would take me as I am.

The heart of man is very much like the sea, it has its storms, it has its tides and in its depths it has its pearls too.

The only time I feel alive is when I'm painting.

I am still far from being what I want to be, but with God's help I shall succeed.

So often, a visit to a bookshop has cheered me, and reminded me that there are good things in the world.

To suffer without complaint is the only lesson we have to learn in this life.

Someday death will take us to another star.

I can't change the fact that my paintings don't sell. But the time will come when people will recognize that they are worth more than the value of the paints used in the picture.

"

I will not live without love.

"

Your profession is not what brings home your weekly pay check, your profession is what you're put here on earth to do, with such passion and such intensity that it becomes spiritual in calling.

The sunflower is mine, in a way.

In the end we shall have had enough of cynicism, scepticism and humbug, and we shall want to live more musically.

If you don't have a dog--at least one--there is not necessarily anything wrong with you, but there may be something wrong with your life.

In spite of everything, I shall rise again; I will take up my pencil, which I have forsaken in my great discouragement, and I will go on with my drawing.

"

I'm such a nobody.

"

Let us keep courage and try to be patient and gentle. And let us not mind being eccentric, and make distinction between good and evil.

Only when I fall do I get up again.

I experience a period of frightening clarity in those moments when nature is so beautiful. I am no longer sure of myself, and the paintings appear as in a dream.

When I have a terrible need of - shall I say the word - religion, then I go out and paint the stars.

Admire as much as you can. Most people do not admire enough.

It is a pity that, as one gradually gains experience, one loses one's youth.

"

I feel such a creative force in me: I am convinced that there will be a time when, let us say, I will make something good every day, on a regular basis....

"

But for one's health as you say, it is very necessary to work in the garden and see the flowers growing.

I think that I still have it in my heart someday to paint a bookshop with the front yellow and pink in the evening...like a light in the midst of the darkness.

And when I read, and really I do not read so much, only a few authors, - a few men that I discovered by accident - I do this because they look at things in a broader, milder and more affectionate way than I do, and because they know life better, so that I can learn from them.

Don't lose heart if it's very difficult at times, everything will come out all right and nobody can in the beginning do as he wishes.

Keep your love of nature, for that is the true way to understand art more and more.

If one feels the need of something grand, something infinite, something that makes one feel aware of God, one need not go far to find it. I think that I see something deeper, more infinite, more eternal than the ocean in the expression of the eyes of a little baby when it wakes in the morning and coos or laughs because it sees the sun shining on its cradle.

As we advance in life it becomes more and more difficult, but in fighting the difficulties the inmost strength of the heart is developed.

What color is in a picture, enthusiasm is in life.

Let's not forget that the little emotions are the great captains of our lives and we obey them without realizing it.

If you work with love and intelligence, you develop a kind of armour against people's opinions, just because of the sincerity of your love for nature and art. Nature is also severe and, to put it that way, hard, but never deceives and always helps you to move forward.

It always strikes me, and it is very peculiar, that, whenever we see the image of indescribable and unutterable desolation—of loneliness, poverty, and misery, the end and extreme of things— the thought of God comes into one's mind.

I shouldn't precisely have chosen madness if there had been any choice, but once such a thing has taken hold of you, you can't very well get out of it.

We spent our whole lives in unconscious exercise of the art of expressing our thoughts with the help of words.

Success is sometimes the outcome of a whole string of failures.

Seek only light and freedom and do not immerse yourself too deeply in the worldly mire.

The lamps are burning and the starry sky is over it all.

There is but one Paris and however hard living may be here, and if it became worse and harder even—the French air clears up the brain and does good—a world of good.

Let me stop there, but my God, how beautiful Shakespeare is, who else is as mysterious as he is; his language and method are like a brush trembling with excitement and ecstasy. But one must learn to read, just as one must learn to see and learn to live.

What preys on my mind is simply this one question: what am I good for, could I not be of service or use in some way?

There was a sentence in your letter that struck me, "I wish I were far away from everything, I am the cause of all, and bring only sorrow to everybody, I alone have brought all this misery on myself and others." These words struck me because that same feeling, just the same, not more nor less, is also on my conscience.

In my view, I am often immensely rich, not in money, but (although just now perhaps not all the time) rich because I have found my metier, something I can devote myself to heart and soul and that gives inspiration and meaning to my life.

I see paintings or drawings in the poorest cottages, in the dirtiest corners. And my mind is driven towards these things with an irresistible momentum.

Do not quench your inspiration and your imagination; do not become the slave of your model.

" We are surrounded by poetry on all sides... **"**

Though I am often in the depths of misery, there is still calmness, pure harmony and music inside me.

I often think of you all, one cannot do what one wants in life.

The more you feel attached to a spot, the more ruthlessly you are compelled to leave it, but the memories remain, and one remembers - as in a looking glass, darkly - one's absent friends.

How right it is to love flowers and the greenery of pines and ivy and hawthorn hedges; they have been with us from the very beginning.

I long so much to make beautiful things. But beautiful things require effort and disappointment and perseverance.

"

If I cease searching, then, woe is me, I am lost. That is how I look at it - keep going, keep going come what may.

"

We feel lonely now and then and long for friends and think we should be quite different and happier if we found a friend of whom we might say: "He is the one." But you, too, will begin to learn that there is much self-deception behind this longing; if we yielded too much to it, it would lead us from the road.

How rich art is, if one can only remember what one has seen, one is never empty of thoughts or truly lonely, never alone.

Both she and I have grief enough and trouble enough, but as for regrets – neither of us have any.

An artist needn't be a clergyman or a church warden, but he must have a warm heart for his fellow men.

The more ugly, old, nasty, ill, and poor I become the more I want to get my own back by producing vibrant, well-arranged, radiant colour.

It's better to have a gay life of it than to commit suicide.

To do good work one must eat well, be well housed, have one's fling from time to time, smoke one's pipe, and drink one's coffee in peace.

It is not only by one's impulses that one achieves greatness, but also by patiently filing away the steel wall that separates what one feels from what one is capable of doing.

The world concerns me only in so far as I have a certain debt and duty to it, because I have lived in it for thirty years and owe to it to leave behind some souvenir in the shape of drawings and paintings – not done to please any particular movement, but within which a genuine human sentiment is expressed.

The more you love, the more you suffer.

I work as diligently on my canvases as the labourers do in their fields.

That I was not suited to commerce or academic study in no way proves that I should also be unfit to be a painter.

"

I take great care of myself by carefully shutting myself away.

"

So what do you want? Does what happens inside show on the outside? There is such a great fire in one's soul, and yet nobody ever comes to warm themselves there, and passersby see nothing but a little smoke coming from the top of the chimney, and go on their way.

"

Sometimes, dear brother, I know so well what I want.

"

It must be good to die in the knowledge that one has done some truthful work...and to know that, as a result, one will live on in the memory of at least a few and leave a good example for those who come after.

I am not an adventurer by choice but by fate.

Life itself, too, is forever turning an infinitely vacant, dispiriting blank side towards man on which nothing appears, any more than it does on a blank canvas. But no matter how vacant and vain, how dead life may appear to be, the man of faith, of energy, of warmth, who knows something, will not be put off so easily.

The victory one would gain after a whole life of work and effort is better than one that is gained sooner.

To understand blue you must first understand yellow and orange.

Be careful not to become narrow-minded, or afraid of reading what is well written, quite the contrary, such writings are a source of comfort in life.

I can very well do without God both in my life and in my painting, but I cannot, suffering as I am, do without something which is greater than I, which is my life, the power to create.

And the memories of all we have loved stay and come back to us in the evening of our life. They are not dead but sleep, and it is well to gather a treasure of them.

Modern reality has got such a hold on us that... when we attempt to reconstruct the ancient days in our thoughts...the minor events of our lives tear us away from our meditations, and... thrust us back into our personal.

Fortunately for me, I know well enough what I want, and am basically utterly indifferent to the criticism that I work to hurriedly. In answer to that, I have done some things even more hurriedly these last few days.

I hope to depart in no other way than looking back with love and wistfulness and thinking, oh paintings that I would have made...

She and I are two unhappy ones who keep together and carry our burdens together, and in this way unhappiness is changed to joy, and the unbearable becomes bearable.

I wanted to make people think of a totally different way of living from that which we, educated people, live. I would absolutely not want anyone to find it beautiful or good without a thought.

There are two ways of reasoning about painting: how to do it and how not to do it; how to do it with great deal of drawing and not much colour, how not to do it with a great deal of colour and not much drawing.

...a woman does not grow old as long as she loves & is loved.

Illusions may fade, but the sublime remains.

The earth from afar shines like a star.

I have tried to express the idea that the café is a place where one can ruin oneself, go mad, or commit a crime.

The cure for him would be to take a good long look at some potato plants, which have lately had such a deep and distinctive colour and tone, instead of driving himself mad looking at pieces of yellow satin and gold leather.

Love is something eternal... The aspect may change but not the essence.

One begins by plaguing oneself to no purpose in order to be true to nature, and one concludes by working quietly from one's own palette alone, and then nature is the result.

"

What would be of life if we didn't have the courage of doing something new?

"

Future generations will probably be able to enlighten us on this very interesting subject, and then science itself—with all due respect—may reach conclusions that are more or less in keeping with Christ's sayings about the other half of our life.

When I see how several painters I know here are struggling with their watercolours and paintings so that they can't see a solution anymore, I sometimes think: Friend, the fault is in your drawing. I don't regret for a moment that I did not go in for watercolour and oil painting straight away. I am sure I will catch up if only I struggle on, so that my hand does not waver in drawing and perspective.

What I am in the eyes of most people - a nonentity, an eccentric, or an unpleasant person - somebody who has no position in society and will never have; in short, the lowest of the low. All right, then - even if that were absolutely true, then I should like to show by my work what such an eccentric, such a nobody, has in his heart.

Drawing is the root of everything!

“

"

One must seize the reality of one's fate and that's that.

"

HOW difficult it is to be simple!

In spite of everything I shall rise again: I will take up my pencil, which I have forsaken in my great discouragement, and I will go on with my drawing.

"

That God of the clergymen, He is for me as dead as a doornail. But am I an atheist for all that?

"

It is better to be high-spirited, even though one makes more mistakes, than to be narrow-minded and all too prudent.

Poetry surrounds us everywhere, but putting it on paper is, alas, not so easy as looking at it.

The thing has already taken form in my mind before I start it. The first attempts are absolutely unbearable. I say this because I want you to know that if you see something worthwhile in what I am doing, it is not by accident but because of real direction and purpose.

"" I believe so. ... Don't accuse anybody else. ""

I have often neglected my appearance. I admit it, and I also admit that it is "shocking."

What is true is that I have at times earned my own crust of bread, and at other times a friend has given it to me out of the goodness of his heart. I have lived whatever way I could, for better or for worse, taking things just as they came.

I must continue to follow the path I take now.

So please don't think that I am renouncing anything, I am reasonably faithful in my unfaithfulness and though I have changed, I am the same, and what preys on my mind is simply this one question: what am I good for, could I not be of service or use in some way, how can I become more knowledgeable and study some subject or other in depth?

Well, right now it seems that things are going very badly for me, have been doing so for some considerable time, and may continue to do so well into the future.

I think that everything that is really good and beautiful, the inner, moral, spiritual and sublime beauty in men and their works, comes from God, and everything that is bad and evil in the works of men and in men is not from God, and God does not approve of it.

Such a one does not always know what he can do, but he nevertheless instinctively feels, I am good for something! My existence is not without reason!

People are often unable to do anything, imprisoned as they are in I don't know what kind of terrible, terrible, oh such terrible cage.

Is all this illusion, imagination? I don't think so. And then one asks: My God! will it be for long, will it be for ever, will it be for eternity?

Do you know what makes the prison disappear? Every deep, genuine affection. Being friends, being brothers, loving, that is what opens the prison, with supreme power, by some magic force. Without these one stays dead. But whenever affection is revived, there life revives.

It constantly remains a source of disappointment to me that my drawings are not yet what I want them to be. The difficulties are indeed numerous and great, and cannot be overcome at once.

A weaver who has to direct and to interweave a great many little threads has no time to philosophize about it, but rather he is so absorbed in his work that he doesn't think but acts, and he feels how things must go more than he can explain it.

Love always brings difficulties, that is true, but the good side of it is that it gives energy.

Aren't the wise ones, those who never do anything foolish, even more foolish in my eyes than I am in theirs?

To some, woman is heresy and diabolical. To me she is just the opposite.

I tell you, if one wants to be active, one must not be afraid of going wrong, one must not be afraid of making mistakes now and then. Many people think that they will become good just by doing no harm — but that's a lie, and you yourself used to call it that. That way lies stagnation, mediocrity.

Life itself, too, is forever turning an infinitely vacant, dispiriting blank side towards man on which nothing appears, any more than it does on a blank canvas. But no matter how vacant and vain, how dead life may appear to be, the man of faith, of energy, of warmth, who knows something, will not be put off so easily.

There is no blue without yellow and without orange, and if you put in blue, then you must put in yellow, and orange too, mustn't you? Oh well, you will tell me that what I write to you are only banalities.

Let's not forget that the little emotions are the great captains of our lives and we obey them without realizing it.

When we are working at a difficult task and strive after a good thing, we are fighting a righteous battle, the direct reward of which is that we are kept from much evil. As we advance in life it becomes more and more difficult, but in fighting the difficulties the inmost strength of the heart is developed.

I feel a certain calm. There is safety in the midst of danger. What would life be if we had no courage to attempt anything?

Some good must come by clinging to the right. Conscience is a man's compass, and though the needle sometimes deviates, though one often perceives irregularities in directing one's course by it, still one must try to follow its direction.

Here are things which we feel to be good and true, though in the cold light of reason and calculation many things remain incomprehensible and dark.

Vincent van Gogh
1853-1890

Paintings from Vincent van Gogh

- *Beach at Scheveningen in Stormy Weather*
- *The 'Laakmolen' near The Hague*
- *Girl in White in the Woods*
- *Lying Cow*
- *A Girl in the Street, Two Coaches in the Background*
- *Cows in the Meadow*
- *Farmhouses Among Trees*
- *Bulb Fields*
- *Drawbridge in Nieuw-Amsterdam*
- *Old Church Tower at Nuenen*
- *Congregation Leaving the Reformed Church in Nuenen*
- *Cart with Black Ox*
- *Cart with Red and White Ox*
- *Avenue of Poplars in Autumn*
- *Still Life with Straw Hat*
- *The Potato Eaters*
- *Skull of a Skeleton with Burning Cigarette*
- *Vase with Red Poppies*
- *Poppy Flowers*
- *Wheat Field with a Lark*
- *View of Paris from Vincent's Room in the Rue Lepic*
- *Portrait of Père Tanguy*
- *A Woman Walking in a Garden*
- *Imperial Fritillaries in a Copper Vase*
- *Agostina Segatori Sitting in the Café du Tambourin*
- *Landscape with Snow*
- *La Mousmé*
- *The Zouave*
- *The Night Café*
- *The Yellow House*
- *Van Gogh's Chair*
- *Café Terrace at Night*
- *Starry Night Over the Rhône*
- *Portrait of the Artist's Mother*
- *Bedroom in Arles*
- *Falling Autumn Leaves*

- *L'Arlésienne*
- *The Red Vineyard*
- *Memory of the Garden at Etten (Ladies of Arles)*
- *Les Arènes*
- *Interior of a Restaurant in Arles*
- *A Lane near Arles*
- *View of Arles, Flowering Orchards*
- *Arles: View from the Wheat Fields*
- *Sunset at Montmajour*
- *Crab on its Back*
- *Two Crabs*
- *La Berceuse*
- *Irises*
- *The Starry Night*
- *Self-portrait (1889)*
- *Self-portrait without beard*
- *Self-Portrait with Bandaged Ear*
- *A Meadow in the Mountains: Le Mas de Saint-Paul*
- *Enclosed Field with Peasant*
- *Green Wheat Field with Cypress*
- *Ivy*
- *Farmhouse in Provence*
- *Road with Cypress and Star*
- *At Eternity's Gate*
- *Thatched Cottages and Houses*
- *Portrait of Dr. Gachet*
- *Doctor Gachet's Garden in Auvers*
- *Houses at Auvers*
- *White House at Night*
- *Girl in White*
- *The Church at Auvers*
- *Daubigny's Garden*
- *Farms near Auvers*
- *The Town Hall at Auvers*
- *Blossoming Chestnut Branches*
- *Peasant Woman Against a Background of Wheat*
- *View of the Asylum and Chapel of Saint-Rémy*
- *Wheatfield with Crows*
- *Tree Roots*
- *Still Life: Vase with Pink Roses*

Vincent van Gogh

Free...

Receive a Kindle Edition in the series for FREE...

Sign up at
www.the secret libraries.com

Find us on:

The Secret Libraries

Published by The Secret Libraries for 2017
www.theSECRETlibraries.com

All rights reserved.
Copyright © 2017

Copyright © 2017

For more information please find us at:

www.theSecretlibraries.com

Thank you for your purchase.

Made in the USA
Monee, IL
01 September 2022

13068574R00095